In Plenty's Woods

BRENDAN GALVIN

In Plenty's Woods

POEMS

Louisiana State University Press
BATON ROUGE

Published by Louisiana State University Press
lsupress.org

Copyright © 2025 by the Estate of Brendan Galvin
All rights reserved. Except in the case of brief quotations used in articles or reviews, no part of this publication may be reproduced or transmitted in any format or by any means without written permission of Louisiana State University Press.

LSU Press Paperback Original

Designer: Kaelin Chappell Broaddus
Typeface: Pliego

Cover illustration courtesy Naya Na/Adobe Stock.

Thanks to the editors of the following publications, in which some of these poems first appeared, some in earlier versions: *Alaska Quarterly Review, Boston College Magazine, Canary: A Literary Journal of the Environmental Crisis, Chronicles, Cortland Review, Gettysburg Review, Greensboro Review, Hibernian Review, Hudson Review, Ibbetson Street, Idaho Review, Missouri Review, Plume, Post Road, Reading Ireland, The Recorder (Journal of the American Irish Historical Society)*, and *Tar River Poetry*.

Library of Congress Cataloging-in-Publication Data

Names: Galvin, Brendan, author.
Title: In plenty's woods : poems / Brendan Galvin.
Description: Baton Rouge : Louisiana State University Press, 2025.
Identifiers: LCCN 2025018343 (print) | LCCN 2025018344 (ebook) | ISBN 978-0-8071-8476-9 (paperback) | ISBN 978-0-8071-8579-7 (epub) | ISBN 978-0-8071-8580-3 (pdf)
Subjects: LCGFT: Poetry
Classification: LCC PS3557.A44 I5 2025 (print) | LCC PS3557.A44 (ebook) | DDC 811/.54—dc23/eng/20250613
LC record available at https://lccn.loc.gov/2025018343
LC ebook record available at https://lccn.loc.gov/2025018344

For Anne and Harold

If you wish to understand the Creator,
first try to understand his creation.
— ST. COLUMBAN

CONTENTS

- I
  - Opening Day 3
  - Looking down Both Barrels 5
  - Plenty's Woods 7
  - Afterwards 8
  - October Snow 9
  - Winterizing 10
  - The Bealaclugga Road 11
  - Deer Week 13
  - Foraging 14

- II
  - Watching the News 17
  - Deepdive EKG 19
  - For a Few Moments of Silence 20
  - Collecting Nests 21
  - A Few Matters of Disposition in the August Garden 22
  - An October Almanac 23

- III
  - Before the Wolf Moon 27
  - Nomad 28
  - Vocab Quiz around the Hummingbird Feeder 29
  - Here on Our Flyway It Must Be April 30
  - Ghost Wrens? 31
  - When I Looked Up Scoldemore 32

- IV
  - You Were Music 35

- V
  - Lughnasa 45
  - Elegy with Birds 46
  - A Donegal Elegy 47
  - Elegy for a Landscaper 48
  - To a Fawn Wandering the Cemetery 49

VI	To a Lone Hitchhiker of the 1950s 53
	Never a Transfer Station, Forever a Town Dump 55
	A Cape Cod Baptism 56
	Tiny Judson and Aunt Mary 58
	Home Cooking 59
	Sawyers 60

VII	Rickety as I Am 63
	Those Backdrop Cities 64
	Porky's Boy 65
	Envy 66
	Under the Wolf Moon 67
	I Will Not Die in Paris on a Thursday 68
	Against Expendables 69

I

Opening Day

When that wren flew under
the top of my propane tank outside
and I saw straw sticking out
I wondered why I had never thought
that could happen, or why I wanted to live
in a house on a dirt road through
a forest like this. A two-day roarer in the pines
had ended without my losing any,
though I watched them leaning,
trying to leave town. But apparently
while my back was turned
the forsythia exploded itself open.
Soon that yellow will be as commonplace
as the white shingles it fronts all over
the county, and now the nuthatches can begin
their annual chase. A chickadee adds
a silhouette to the pine shadows. Soon the Asian
pear trees will be offering white bouquets
to the new sky, and it won't be long
before a rubythroat will be after
the hanging sugar-water the sun is
treating the way it treats this
untrimmed splash of forsythia. Rain
will lift that water to the hummer's thirst,
and the grandfather apple tree
I opened a hole for over fifty years ago,
knotted and spindly now, like me,
will flower last as usual. Is this
what they call plenitude? A grosbeak
without color, maybe pregnant,
sits on a railing for the evening,
as unrecognizable to me as that wren.

A trout lily in blossom, sent in a seed
from who knows where, nods in agreement
like a tiny dutch-girl doll
at the edge of the walkway.

Looking down Both Barrels

A beach walker now, I check on
the harbor seals and grays, the eiders
and an occasional humpback.
I also greet Lefty, Finnbarr, Magnus,
Patches, Ollie, Amber the size
of an elk, Eartha, Hamish, Peanut—

more dogs in this town
than Obie, Dubber, Sally, and Tink,
who might also have been dogs
except they are people under stones
in several of these green hills.

Even Scotty, who advised me
to try and check out before I turned
eighty and non-negotiable things
found me, is under stone.

Too late, Scotty, too late.

That I walk like a penguin
is only arthritis, one of my four
medical practitioners promises,
and not ataxia, a word that, whole
or in parts, raises suspicions.

And the myelodysplastic goings-on
would sound like yodeling,
except it's in my bones and blood,
the iron of which they tell me
is a gift of my Celtic inheritance.

So this is how eighty looks,
clutching not a shillelagh
but a blackthorn walking stick
cut from the floor of Sassy Bryan
McLaughlin's unthatched cottage.

I call it my Ballyloskey Slugger,
but don't be afraid. It's only
for keeping my pelvic region
on the straight and narrow
as I walk the edge of a DPW gouge
here at ocean side. They say

the Icelandic fishing captains
could dream where the big schools were,
but these days all I can do
is wait for April rains to fill this ditch—
far from a vernal pool—

with murk that draws
the plip, plip of a few frogs,
and the cloudlike conceptions
of salamanders, indicators
that things might continue
another season or more.

Plenty's Woods

In this pitch-piney corner there are
no bears, but this morning
down by the little pond where
blue herons sometimes pose
and the odd river otter may design
a bullseye on the surface,
at the tip of a ruined pine was
an osprey, off the wing, feet
clasping a white fish belly.
Same one I saw years ago,
or its twin with the same
claw-hammer head, taking its
time, casual, pecking its catch into
a casualty before cleaning itself
like a cat. Definitely not the same one
that blows the equipment, leaving
three towns of us without power
for an hour at a time. And around here
a Portuguese man-of-war isn't
a ship or a pirate, but you don't
want to swim near its tentacles
or flip it over onshore with a bare foot.
The coyote this afternoon is
casual, too. Meandering uphill
from the marsh on property I call
mine and he no doubt thinks of
as his, stopping to mark a blue tarp,
then on to lap from my garden pool.
I've seen the scat around here,
and my dog Lefty sniffing
the grass clumps out, and the coyote
headed across the road to
my neighbor's coop,
intent on casualties of his own.

Afterwards

Quite clearly from a dream that first night home
you cried out, "I can't see the avocados!"
But I didn't understand what that truly meant
until I brought you to the Produce Barn
and you went for the fruit
as though after a year in steerage
instead of your time in Heron Pond Rehab.
You negotiated like a first waltz lesson
the aisle of citruses, loose apples,
and plums lit up like a carnival midway.
That was after I drove a few of
the back roads so I could prove to you
that this town hadn't changed in your absence—
Black Pond Road, East Bayview, Old County,
Spectacle Creek. Only then could you inhale
the scents of pocked melons again, squeezing,
testing with your good hand for ripenesses
like a woman getting ready to bowl.
Then filling the cart with colors and smells,
the juices of this world. Terrified
for your balance, I grabbed
that handle with both hands.

October Snow

First flakes, and now before they gather
to a whiteness, the chickadees and
redbreast nuthatches take turns
at my hummingbird feeder, meaning
to stay, not disappearing
as the hummers did,
following the orioles who fled
their empty orange halves.
These flurries seem the drift of
broken light across the air, a minute-
to-minute covering that's spare
and quiet, the opposite of night.
Where once I watched, I stand alone
and see new things—
the beachplum bushes whitely
blossoming, or so it seems.
I think of the migrants, hope
for them in their winter crossings,
dangers of mountains and predators,
deserts, though I cannot calculate
how many days and night flights
the stars direct, wind strengths
or the planet's magnetic fields,
low frequency sound waves,
and whose body clocks advise
their taking leave, or who spreads wings
for the scent of ocean. At my feeder,
meaning to stay, the chickadees
and nuthatches take turns
dipping their bills more than once
to prove the water is still water.

Winterizing

Aspen are one sign, their leaf flocks
flying in place, a gold-foil panic
as juices migrate toward
new summers rumored in the roots,

and on the grove's farthest edge,
too quick to name, a helical ascent
up the trunk, lost in the branches,
then a drawn-out inquiry
like the questions of a child.

The juxtapositions: one least sandpiper
against the glossy October ocean,
then houses that seem to have stepped
from their leaves and owned up to
themselves and the nineteenth century.

Yesterday, on the banks of
the Herring River, smartweed was
flowering as if to offer its best
to the whole fall Atlantic in the air.

I think of all the moments no one notices:
the height where a late bean tendril
probing above its stake senses
frost and turns its barb on itself,

and these squash plants that opened
to showers, all elbows and knees,
stiffening now, anxious to
push out their turgid completions.

The Bealaclugga Road

First morning, and I went running early,
barely 6 a.m., getting a wave from
the first farmer heading out on his tractor,
and no notice at all from a field
of huge cows. Corcomroes? Charolais?

I wouldn't know until the day I visited
the ruins of the Cistercian abbey
Cromwell had trashed, at the base
of the Burren's limestone hills where
falcons nested on a standing column.

That day at Corcomroe I found the effigy
of King Conor O'Brien, who neither
waved nor winked, and the seeping well
where the monks' cows had fattened on grass
green as the fields of Limerick
I had flown over into Shannon, greener
than any tale-telling uncle
of mine had ever claimed.

But that first morning, all I'd read was scrambled.
What was the difference between transhumance
and booleying? What was a grike? A turlough?
Only two years later on hands and knees
would I crawl into a passage grave.

But that morning? Was I running past Dog's Mercury
and Irish Eyebright? Clints, nunataks? Clearly
I was learning a new language,
though kamenitzas didn't sound local.

Then from the fog on Ballyvaughan Bay
a shorebird called, drawing me to a stone pier
in the country of my forebears,
nearly in tears. I could not name the bird.

Deer Week

The deer, who I knew would take his time
leaving this grove, and my border collie,
who even on beaches I have to keep
leashed against kissing strangers,
since he loves everyone.

Manny Flores told me
he'd once counted over 100 ticks
in one ear of a buck he'd just shot, but
nobody knew who shot Manny in the back

one deer week, though messing with
another hunter's wife was one way
payback can occur around here. *Frantic Antics
by the Atlantic,* as the scandal sheet put it.
Who knew? And when that happened
who knew Father Medeiros would buy up
all the local copies, protecting his flock?

Foraging

Begin just before Thanksgiving
by the jetty. The flocks of eiders
coming south to winter over
will tell you when, their flights
sounding like some engine
of the earth. Then and there
those scallops the bay washes up
will color the sand like a mosaic of shells.

Since your neighbor goes home to the city each fall,
maybe you've already stuffed your pockets
with apples bright as railroad lanterns
on that tree she's never seen to fruition.

Now the boletes, those variegated mushrooms
in the understories of oak and pine
after hard rains and warm suns, then recovered
with dirt and leaves to preserve
their fine mycelial roots for other years.

Or else begin on the fireroad in July,
that private alcove where the highbush
blueberries thrive, or earlier in the dune lands
where in May the beachplums blossom like
late snow to portend another year
of memorable breakfasts. Have it
your way: start or finish where you will.

Rosehips? Find that woman who lives
by the tides and calendar in your town, and notes
on paper scraps how much sugar goes where,
what to sprinkle with grated cheese, where
a teaspoon of tapioca is needed, when to add
the walnuts or a handful of cranberries.
She knows where the rosehips grow.

II

Watching the News

A second mug of French roast and I woke up
to the deer's head topping my TV
like a threat in a Mafia movie,
and then, thank God, the flexing ears,
fifty feet away in the yard,
maybe checking out my own head
from the wire side of the box, as well as
hearing the broadcast it may have believed
I was delivering. Seeing is believing
the biggest mammal in these woods,
then at the red plastic flower
I'd filled with sugar and water out there,
the smallest bird, nearly dragonfly size,
rubythroat, returned from Panama
and not inclined to go farther away than
the scrub oaks, loving the flower's taste.
This is the news around here, what goes on,
the daily pastoral surprise, the blue
heron solitude, this and the two fawns
I see some evenings on Rose's Hill,
their long scuts flicking with pleasure,
their heads deep in grass. They feed like cattle
on the far side of the marsh, driven from
deeper cover where coyotes den this time of year.
Early one morning a fawn so new it couldn't
manage any two legs at once
trailed a doe down from Rose's Hill to drink
in the pond, but I have seen two wolf-sized curs
scouting that hill before skulking back into the trees,
and those two yearlings like rangy colts faking
around each other over there, bucking,
for a quarter hour putting moves on each other
in the teeth of mortality. The news is all in the timing,
all in being here, the long looking. I have already

seen Muckle Flugga, so why should I see
Paris before I die? Even heard the cottontail's scream,
which I thought was folklore, cried out
as my unknowing dog stood over it, unwilling.

Deepdive EKG

Heartsounds. Like recorded fishburps
when that technician held her mike
to my left side. Submarine wooshing
from the benthic level,
the sea things breathing out down there
where the vegetation hangs on
in waves, grows in wild gray
hedges over stones, and hides
the schoolmaster, a fish tasty but
risky and a poor swimmer,
or else the throbbing Atlantic stargazer,
electric organs behind his eyes,
or some other gargler predatory
in habit, who lives in the Garden of
the Queen off Cuba's coast, but who can
live long under refrigeration as well?
Certainly not the swelling gigantic
wreckfish, dweller in caves
and hull remnants, blowing threats
as if from a hose, but maybe
the *Tridacna maxima*, giant mollusk
of the Asian oceans. Or else a houting,
not yet fried or smoked,
or perhaps a painted comber of
the rocky bottoms, the lone defender
of its waters, or a small rainbow runner
that would make good sashimi.
Flushes, sounds fishes might make
in water, a Dorab wolf-herring
woofing a warning, not just a game to kill
the hour that microphone patrolled
the shoals and currents, maybe even
the mesopelagic reaches of my blood.

For a Few Moments of Silence

Out of that gray two hundred miles
between Iceland and Mykines
a pair of turnstones arrived and landed
on the stern rail close by, resting
while I tried to grow into
a silence like theirs.

More listener these days than talker,
a childhood in the blueberry barrens
and pineys grows stronger in me
each year than anything the airwaves
can pitch at me. I'd have to live
among islands and seal pastures a longer time

to connect with their quiet, and stop
envying the stillness those first seafarers
to the New World must have occupied
on deck after hints from a breeze
of earth and wildflowers
they couldn't yet see.

The turnstones peel off south
toward winter in Africa, leaving me with
the thought of those Old World mariners
hearing the quirks of a clinker-built craft
calling them back to its handling.

Collecting Nests

I stood with the grass turning around
my knees, and the bushes whose maroon haze
signified their readiness to begin again,
a few natural egg cups woven in them
here and there, abandoned or waiting.
Lighter than any teacup-sized nest
a warbler would build, a hummingbird's
saddle on the merest knuckle of an apple tree
looked more like a ring on the hand
of Dame Edith Sitwell. Was this
the year I'd find borrowed strands from a dogtail
woven among the twigs? Strips from a defrocked
snakeskin? Perhaps silver tinsel from
a lost Christmas? Alerted to the distant voices
of crows, I thought Celan was wrong about
The Nowhere of nests. What of the architectural skills
displayed by the orioles' sacks, and those
pickup sticks lined with bark, leafage, and chips,
packed with dried mud
that incorporated weeds, things Celan
would consider litter or mulch?
Whatever a woodcock could scrape
together, and the piling of duck down
on straw? Each year I hunt before
the eggs are laid. The birds have an eye
and brain for whatever is useful to assure
their generations. If there is no horsetail
they can always look for a dog.

A Few Matters of Disposition
in the August Garden

Their blossoms distract like
the pout on Mae West, so the beans
can be hard to see at first.
Just stand here awhile, until
you can ignore even the Dumbo ears
of squash in all this green tangle,

and begin to see the cannellini,
romanos, and emperors
you will have to pick before
the frosts cure them to leather.

If a buzzing and crackling occurs
it's probably that insect you see
two or three times a summer,
and suggests that technology
has designed and miniaturized it
for collecting information.

If this happens in August, when
the squash plants have vaulted the fence,
you may think that Voltaire was wrong,
that history will track us down,
even into our gardens. Use the longest
unoccupied beanpole to part the canopy

and peer into the understory, wary
of disturbing the acorn squashes
and pattypans, the zucchinis and crooknecks,
an occupant of your century looking for
the improvised explosive device.

An October Almanac

That nameless tint hovering above sunset
a few evenings, just shy
of the conflagration, has bequeathed
itself to the sickle asters now. Rich
with it, they foam up everywhere,
largesse in the glower of a hunter's moon
that aims to change everything. Poison
ivy's taken off up trees and down ditches,
in robbery or elopement carrying away
those last western lights that bleed out into
darkness. Now deer have traded their coats
with cinnamon ferns, in exchange for
the marshes' weathered brindle.
This morning, where their track angles
down out of the high woods
to the drinking place at the river,
signs of a scuffle that churned the path
to dirt. The dog noses there, eyes doleful
with last night's story: late, the world
gone black and white, a face, briefly
between trees, then faces wild to cancel barter.

III

Before the Wolf Moon

Are you early or late? That's
what my father used to ask
when I dragged home sticky
and oiled from spraying roads
with asphalt, and what I want
to ask a yellow-throated warbler
as rain on my woodpile tarps
thickens to ice.

If it snows
again tonight the cardinal's
suit of flame won't even warm
imagination, but I'll rise early
tomorrow and hang a chunk of suet
for that yellow-throated one
who's lighter and more fleeting
than my pocket change,
and too far north to be delving
into pinecones for sustenance.

Come January, the locals will be
vocalizing in tangles of underbrush
and oak scrub, and hanging, feeding
on my rewards, or scrambling their flocks
like winged ampersands against the raptors,
and this yellow-throated southerner
will amount to a single week logged into
a field manual a half-century old.

Nomad

Even in snow like this,
best to wait the occasional bird out,
let it get back to balance and eyesight if it can,
watch it work its neck as a downy
woodpecker might, or raise itself and take off
for a branch it knows it can reach, away
from predators. Or else freeze
on its belly and remain awhile
as I've seen an ovenbird do
until late in the day,
when I checked and it was gone.
This bird was not usual, however,
never had I seen its dark green back
among darker feathers and white-striped
wings before. What I could do
not to frighten it into another problem
was wait all afternoon until I was sure
it was done for, then flip it with
a grandchild's shovel. Whatever it was,
it had flown against a window reflection
it had taken for the woods. Crossbill,
obviously, not red like its cousin, but that evening
I looked up the white-winged ones, found
this gray-green female, vagrant maybe
from the high Maritimes. I read how
white-wings sometimes flew south to pick seeds
out of pitch pines they considered useless,
but only when they ran out of hemlock seeds
at home. Did hunger deliver her to us,
as the states below sometimes sent
a painted bunting or Bachman's sparrow?
I thought how poetry, like snow,
can work against the commonplace.

Vocab Quiz around the Hummingbird Feeder

First Saturday in May and it's back,
but from my angle only the silhouette,
looking for its feeder, a red plastic
flower under the bench all winter,
and dirty, needing to spend
this afternoon in the sink, while I find
the brown sugar and the cheese grater
to reduce it from rocks to powder
and mix a fresh jar of sweet water.

If there's one bird I wish I could
speak to it's this one, to find out
what country or island it wintered in
this year. Every May I wonder
if there's someone down there
as anxious as I am, watching a feeder,
waiting like a beloved relative,
but I'd have to engage in therianthropy
as the sealfolk do, or in my case
the hummerfolk, to ask it
what blossoms it has stuck that
needle-nose in since last fall.

It won't be long before an ant safari
carries my goodies away, or rain
collects in a feeder puddle
so an oriole stops by for a quick one.
Or else a night raccoon knocks
everything to the deck and guzzles it.
Therianthropy, Alphitomancy? Any wonder
the jocks who majored in tooth-brushing
at school used to call me Big Word Baby?

Here on Our Flyway It Must Be April

Although one winter junco is bug-hunting
in the weedy mud, and for days a crazy robin
has defended its nesting place against

itself in the trapezoidal window
where last year a yellowthroat
attacked its bandit-masked reflection.

Other springs a towhee buffeted
the glass, but now the outer world
is busy as arrivals from the south

turn the garden pool splashy with joy
and a pine warbler does its sewing-machine
imitation somewhere in the trees.

Inside it's noisy. Lefty's barking again
at the TV weight-loss woman whose voice
he appears to be in love with. No snowbirds

are back from the Keys yet in pink bermudas
and belts picturing sailboats roundabout,
to mispronounce "scallops" and laugh at

the remains of our woodpiles, and help
vaporize our bees into extinction.
A flicker dings the satellite dish.

Ghost Wrens?

A pair of the Bewick wrens
ornithologists claim have left these
eastern states. Cats and overdevelopment?
Not in this pitchpine forest where a coyote
may stray. One wren's in the scrub oaks,
one's under the cod on my weathervane,
hanging on, both too skinny to be Carolinas,
too tall for winter or marsh wrens,
and both approximating the odd
new song I heard earlier from bed.
Courtship? Or else they came
this far north the way the Swainson's
warblers and swallowtail kites
do now, the Bewicks dodging Fay,
a tropical storm taking her time
to get on up our flyway? Tail cocked,
one drags a creepy-crawly off
the walkway railing. I'll never complain.
This eastern version is rusty red,
so makes the most colorful songs
in their breeding season, birders say.
These brightest ones trill, seem to
scold almost with pleasure, chirr softly,
mimic kids whistling for dogs,
drop buzzes and zees in among
their subjects, verbs, and adjectives
like small electric tools, and drag
it all into complex meditations
no one can translate yet.

When I Looked Up Scoldemore

A bit of social engineering
and they've taken the squawk
out of the old scolder. The index
sent me to see long-tailed duck,
but aren't there other ducks
with long tails? Why didn't it
send me to Musceget duck
or cockawee or another early
moniker, something with
color and texture, singularity,
some backtrack and salt-water
haven attached to it?

Another name extinct before
its bearer. Will the long-tailed duck
tower in flocks above the ocean
spring and fall, rising in circles
out of sight, dropping fast the way
scoldemores used to?

The rufous-sided towhee
is only the eastern towhee now.
What's next on Civility's To-Do List,
the pig pen leech and other fishing flies
reduced to a clip of hair, feather
and hook size, a new name that is
no name? Let's switch the alewife
to pintspouse, the high school football team
from Lancers to Literacy Volunteers.

IV

You Were Music

1.

I could say it began with
your smoky delivery.
That first time you and I
walked down Musselshell Way
together, I knew I was
walking with music. Even when
we climbed the jetty
I could hear it in that breeze.
Songs you sang in the lounges
of Denver and Omaha
followed me on our walk
back to Corn Hill parking lot.

I could hear them on
Stellwagen Bank, too, when
I took you to watch
the humpbacks drive into
their feasts of krill,
and you turned to me with
that smile that made
the waves sing.

2.

When you said, "Oh, God,
I've gone and fallen for
a poet who watches birds
and bakes his own bread,"
I was happy as a woodchuck
living in a forest all his own.
Hang-gliding over the playgrounds
between our ears, the things
we told each other!

When I looked at the sky
some evenings, I was loving you
so much I knew you were
seeing the same sunset two hundred
miles away. What more
did we need to prove that
we had a weird circuitry with
the universe? Our emails
and phone calls zero minutes apart?

3. Advice

If it comes to asking the mirror
what you could look like in ten years,
punch yeasted dough on a lightly floured
surface instead, and roll it into a loaf.
Bake bread: carraway rye, potato,
honey whole wheat with cranberries,
maybe nine-grain. Recall the mothers
and grandmothers of Clearview
and you will remember how.
A couple of hours to rise
in a warm place, then the oven.
Maybe you'll dream around
in a lifetime of bakeries then, Yoder's
on Ferry Street or the Boulangerie Girardin
on St. Pierre, or else wake in the dark
to the fragrance of a loaf
you made in the kitchen today.
Now it is roaming the house, maybe gone
as far as inspecting the pump and furnace,
and passing through guest room curtains
to reconstitute itself among books, flattening out
over bags of winter clothing, shoaling and
thinning from one room to the next,

for sixteen hours flowing and streaming until
it finds you way up there in the top of the house.
In that late, aromatic dark you will
sleep as deeply as a child.

4.

One night you called to tell me
that in another dimension
there may still be milkmen
delivering from horsecarts,
and paperboys watching
pigeons crossing dawn skies.
Or you'd say another night
that the trees are telling the birds
to shut up and take cover in this wind.

You gave me back my young heart.
Music even in the clang of pans
and pots when you crawled
under the counter to retrieve
the right one and your perfect
subcore was perfect again
in that doorway.

5. Like a Prisoner on *Papillon*

Another morning snow here
on Egg Island, so I feed the woodstove
and think of you drinking coffee
across the barrier water, wishing
as we both do that the ferry was direct,
without a three-state obstacle and sometimes
forbidding weather that spins off
Africa and tracks the Gulf Stream north.

Do we give storms human names and eyes
to personify the control we'll never have,
since they are shape-shifters that could
shave our islands of all our Love
and us in an hour or less? Today I'm
stuck with memories of our first meeting
at the *Mary Ellen*'s off-ramp, when I said,
You're beautiful. It was no lie, though
I'm serving time for it this morning.

6. Courtship

Now the mockingbird sits in the bittersweet,
clear-eyed as a monk, waiting for
the möbius strip of its repertoire,
snapped by the cold, to mend,

and the grounded heron
looks like a negative of a marsh-side
cedar over there, feathers
puffed for insulation. Dr. Zhivago weather,

and nightly now, under the snow moon,
the owls are singing of love and death,
the big-ticket items that leave us
tongue-tied.

Singing the way
they were meant to, in miles of
moonwhite on snow, in leaf scutter
magnified by silence, in the fallen
shadows of trees slain by this moon.

Death or love, his *basso profundo*
across the frozen river leaves no room
for small talk. Then hers, from a farther grove,
I know who you are, too.

Across a serious bay, three states,
and a saltwater sound, may you and I
do as well through these redundant
winter nights. May the sweet talk
of the four of us never falter.

7. Feb.14th

Better than red hearts
full of chocolate, the first
redwinged blackbird is lurking
in the trees, and yesterday
a carolina wren was
fancy-stepping on my
firewood-splitting block.
Mee tooo, mee tooo, whistled
something new in the woods
when I came back from the P.O.

The black-capped, white,
and gray ones are becoming
dull as winter. Sure the cardinals
were red, but the raven never came back.
Now for liberation I recall the February
you carved suet into a heart shape
and slipped it into the feeder,
Love, before I even got out
of bed, and I see that the amaryllis
in the window looks blown
to auricles and ventricles.

8.

These were our easy times.
Music so sweet and tough
the owls inquired for you,
drawn to our bedroom as if
to rabbits. I still wake up
and look for you beside me
the way the soul searches
for all it calls its own.

Then one of your lab tests was
everywhere red. "My world
is physically drifting away," you said.
"Another day, another chemo. There's
no cure, which is unfair to both of us.
Finding us and losing you isn't fair."

9.

You were all the music I ever wanted.
It didn't have to be me standing here
when the sun hit the wild mustard,
but it was, and the breeze
filled suddenly with that weed's
perfume—another moment
that returned when you said
heaven for you meant a library
where you'd read every book
in its own language and understand.

When you left the room, a single crow
lit on a branch outside and practiced
a repertoire of *yawks* and clicks, yelps

and *carrocks,* maybe telling our whole story
to the little creek and its dogwoods
before he tried it on his kind.
You'd have the original *Mabinogion*
in your heaven, if I could choose,
but I'd want that crow, too,
and the veal we ate that first
evening together in Ciro and Sal's.
I'd swap you that for the *Kalevala,*
and the *Book of Ballymote* for another
moment in that yellowing field.
If I could I'd see that *Yenji's Saga*—
all twelve volumes—would be there,
and lost anonymous masterworks,
the Blue Jewel Papyrus, say,
and the Benvali Codex. We would read
them together, but I'd have to insist
on at least one mockingbird
polishing up what a wren just jaggedly
sang, and a mule or two, with whatever
else you'd like. And you.

10. Two Funerals

What Muse had finer legs?
During high school that pastor could forgive
your golf, but read you out for winning
the state public speaking trophy with
the King James version of the 23rd Psalm.

Later all he could ask was, "Are you
trying to turn your father's funeral
into a Broadway show?" Fond
of surprises, you may have drawn on

Phaedra or Daisy Mae or Kate
of *Kiss Me Kate* or another
of your stage roles to discombobulate him,
or did he know I called you Off-Broadway Jo-Jo?

When the bagpiper you flew in from Omaha
started down the aisle in mufti
behind your dad's coffin, you saw the surprise
light your mother's proud head.

Love, you have passed to your father's side.
Nevertheless, I have found a surprise for you, too.
No plaid, no drone, just a small poem at midnight
that you and I didn't know I'd write. It begins,
What Muse had finer legs? And ends when you said,
"I'll be whispering in your ear. Listen for me
between the wind and water."

V

Lughnasa

> Ellen Baer Galvin, 1935–2014

The only whippoorwill in ages
sings to adore the hour. Years ago
that American nightingale
deepened the colors of every
evening's going, and I lay
in fresh pajamas and bath soap,
letting the downstairs adult voices
talk me into the dark the way
Anne as a baby went to sleep
reciting Mama, Papa, naming
even Blackie and Tigger.
Four a.m. is time and voices,
distances and rooms, the surprise
that you were always here among
every thankful thing, and knew
the names of flowers. And let's
praise whatever shadowed us
along the possible side roads
and through the right doors
to Love, that led us to that Deerfield
orchard in bloom, and married us on
August first, the Celtic feast of Lugh,
god of the arts and harvests, and thank
the twin lights of Chanukah and Christmas
as well, that guided us to forty-six
Lughnasa mornings when we woke
to each other's unguarded faces.

Elegy with Birds

Since you are gone, and since
I cannot bring myself to bake
the holiday cookies without you,
I distributed a bag of walnuts first,
then hazelnuts. A red squirrel
zipped across the deck, then
a cardinal redder than any
hanging leaf, and the squirrel
again, this time as though he had
passed from joy into hilarity.

Then the whole almonds drew
the smaller birds you seldom see
on calendars—chickadees,
nuthatches, titmice, one red
crossbill, juncos, sparrows,
each snatching one nut
and fleeing. As though
following arrows, a bluejay
went from nut to nut.

I thought how we used to stir
and press the various nuts
into our dough after concocting it
from the German in your cookbooks,
tags torn from packaging, index cards
and the elegant scripts women
swapped with us, our mutual
Chanukah and Christmas gifts.

9:30 a.m. and the deck is
already clear. This is a love poem
I cannot read to you.

A Donegal Elegy

> A syntax opulent with tomorrows. It is our response
> to mud cabins and a diet of potatoes; our only
> method of replying to . . . inevitabilities.
> —BRIAN FRIEL (1929–2015), *Translations*

Donal McCann onstage, his monologue
the last confession of your faith healer,
Frank Hardy, could make flesh cringe.
Two generations from the plow
and the unschooled, you understood
the tragedy of the local and became
Ireland's Chekhov. Aloof, even arrogant,
the way any private man may be miscast,
you translated the ditches in the common soul
into Irish-English, speech rich with hopes
and futures, tracking the search
for an elusive home between bafflements
and exclusions. With no ridicule you exposed
down to its pagan foundations the truth
of Ballybeg. And thanks for drawing
your Mundy sisters near enough
to my Ballyloskey aunts with their sudden need
to crack for an odd hour that ice
the Vikings had brought down
into Lough Swilly and Lough Foyle.

Elegy for a Landscaper

The holes we find scraped out at the edge
of a paving slab, for instance, so
the cement is a capstone for whatever
goes on beneath. Gary, you knew that lives

go on in those underworlds we are only
conscious of when we hoe around plantings
and discover an entrance, or in a hollow stump
where nobody would risk a hand.

Tree pests, creepers and humpers,
drilling bees, chipmunks, even wood rats
are easily explained, but the mind has
other labyrinths it can populate

the way an Oxford don might furnish
a troll kingdom with everything from warts
to mountaintops down there. These are not
passage graves we can wriggle through
by flashlight to view a stone basin of bones.

Nor would we drink to our diminishment
and enter if we could, as in your way
you did, a laid-off landscaper and veteran
after three rounds of Shock and Awe.

Increasingly wary of human company,
wanting to live among the pines, you chose
a hill beyond town and tunneled for weeks,

strategically poking air holes, and mined
the damp sand to passages and mazes
around the unyielding roots of things,
to end in a bunker the size of a two-car garage.

To a Fawn Wandering the Cemetery

If a butterfly can take on
the image and motions of a soul,
why not you? Who were you once,
a local nicknamed Freddie Eastville
for the way you hitch-hiked home
from work on Route 6, or the tosspot
scalloper Captain Teabag,
or a gas station attendant named
Eddie Skroth? Maybe you're
Mariah Atwood, looking for the grave
of your daughter Lisbeth, or one of
the boys who called themselves
the Piss-cutter Navy, and wrote
love notes in white paint on
the asphalt of back roads. Or perhaps
Police Chief Morton, who once
told them, "If I ever catch you
wringing your mittens again in public,
even at night, it's curtains for you boys."
The Reverend Mary Raymond
visiting her stone is also possible;
then again you could be Tadpole Bell
who returned from the West Coast
wearing ankle boots with silver chains
that rattled when he walked down
Main Street bowlegged as
a cowpuncher. In this town where
everyone from Dr. Wainright
to the boondoggler Smithers has a story,
which was your Love? How many
here are your family, under these
old stones and new? Did you earn
your shape over time for kindnesses
you never mentioned, or fast
as sunlight across a coyote's flank?

VI

To a Lone Hitchhiker of the 1950s

What a piece of work you were
in your seeker's outfit of rundown
desert boots and that dry cleaner's
nightmare of a trenchcoat, publicly
fraying at the wrists and nape,
your frown clenched on the invisible
arrow of pain quivering
between your eyes. Love was
a bad shot then, or your own green
judgment had overdosed on
jukebox ontology, but I'd still
pass you by if I saw you thumbing
in the breakdown lane today,
having heard your lecture about
being your own hero already,
and your beery readings from
On the Road. Find a rut and stay
in it, I'd have to advise, no more
sobbing to motherly bar-flies or that
vacationing priest kind enough
to pull over and let you in
out of the rain. OK, so I'd stop too,
but only to ask how I've lived up
to your expectations. Maybe I'd hit you
with the compost analogy—My boy
(I might say), all life is process:
You take an unpromising fish we call
the pogie, bony and well-oiled,
about as edible as a transistor radio.
But you rake a dead bushel off
the tideline, treat them with buckets of
lobster shell at no cost from the market,
then layer in straw, cowflops, coffee
grounds and rinds, and you have

the start of a green machine. Without
resorting to Voltaire I'd tell you how
you'll learn that nothing's more interesting
than what happens, that we aren't
all on the same schedule. The ineptness
of adults will astonish you. There are
men and women whose vocation's
the equivalent of peddling topsoil
they've padded out with rocks
and so much sand the earth goes blond
at the first hosing. Stop shuddering
every time we pass a roadkill.
Most things you fear aren't going
to happen. Be kinder to yourself.
Seatbelt on, safe by this rolled-up
window at the back of someone's mind,
you grow more like a son every year.
I'll stick my neck out and predict
you'll meet a woman so mutual to
your needs that one of these nights
she'll change your inner weather,
even make you learn to drive. Nothing
is going to please you more than
the moves a sentence makes
on its way down a page: this
you will call the pursuit of happiness.

Never a Transfer Station, Forever a Town Dump

Muddle and rummage, and men
with a special talent
for it. Take Tilton
for starters, drawing on
his White Mule gloves
so slow he won't have to
help you unload,
though the tremors are real,
a used-to-be electrician's
hot-wired palsy. Take
Three Dog, our Man of Yale
who'd tip for the last
brown corner of any bottle,
trying to live himself down,
or Stanley, our master of
misrule, whose puppet
Uncle Sam stood arm-in-arm
with Jesus one year,
with Santa Claus another,
whose concrete deer
stared glass-eyed out at us
from shrubbery, one somehow
a zebra. All to hell
and gone, now that a lady
retired from away recycles
our confusions for
the township. She'll tell
you how to park, where
everything goes. No more
deer to eyeball
a jumpy taxpayer, no more
grasping a doll's head
instead of a doorknob
to enter the swap shop.

A Cape Cod Baptism

That's what they used to call it around here
when a northeaster got the tip of its chisel
into a roof and brought rain in
to travel the joists and form
clouds on the ceiling plaster, then

drip into galvanized buckets and enamel pots
the housewife set around, maybe thinking,
Thank God for gravity: it keeps water
from staying up there and rotting everything.

One time or another, no house here without
its baptism. Which is why from rooftree
to the doubled lines of cedar shakes
that overlap the foundation's red bricks,
the Cape Cod house was built to shed rain
and let wind pass without hindrance.

Now when some washashore buys a classic,
like as not he'll leave just enough wall standing
to soothe the building inspector, or run
a hundred-foot ell off one side so the finished product
looks like a nineteenth-century streetcar barn

topped off with Thoor Ballylee, more angles
and corners than a Rubix cube. Then he'll go
to the river and inquire whether the oysters
are running today, and how many times
the tide will be coming in.

When we drive by his McMansion
decked out to catch views of six different
bodies of fresh and salt water, one of us says,
Looks like Bavaria, all that castle hanging
off the hill, and the other says, Good
candidate for a baptism.

Tiny Judson and Aunt Mary

Was he already bullet-headed
and thickening then, blunt
as in those years when he drove truck
for the town, a seal-shape in
a bachelor's stiff white shirt,
with a pack of Luckies pocketed?

And yet that day enthralled enough
by your contradiction of red hair
and reticence to actually walk up to you
here on Main Street and speak?

I see you reddening deeper into
that fairytale moment a lifetime ago,
teacher, watercolorist,
and Yes, you would meet him
right here that evening.

Sworn to secrecy against
your sisters, my father drove you
into town, and later made me
sole keeper of how
Tiny Judson stood you up.

Because you gave the world
back to itself in pastels, I doubt
you ever figured out that he was
the more fearful that evening.

Had he appeared, what might
have changed for both of you,
I have wondered, but always end
appalled at the power of loneliness
to annul enchantment.

Home Cooking

I would cut my right arm off
for Magdalena Sacco, Foley said
out front of Ernie's Pizza. We were
fifteen, of logic and non-sequitur
knew zero, but raised our eyebrows
to concede First Love. This morning
when I sliced a nine-grain loaf
too deeply with the serrated knife
I thought of that. My thumb pad bled
again. Bagels are toughest, but I
have wrung my hands in aloe
for not using kitchen mitts except
as sock puppets to make you laugh
in your living-room hospital bed.
Your favorite the red-bellied
woodpecker's a regular at the suet
from there, and you can't see me
in your kitchen butchering myself.
Hot skillet handshakes; cuts and nicks.
No microwave exploding veggies
fifty years ago in my bachelor pad.
A few pots boiled to black then, and some
pork chops solid as ashtrays,
but fear was never an ingredient
until the visiting nurses, wheelchair,
brace, this whole endeavor. Love, I will
take more care. I will not cut
my right arm off for you.

Sawyers

I gave Mr. Sawyer a dollar each Saturday
so I could play the violin on loan
from the junior high for him,
which made me a sawyer too,
on the days I practiced, sawing away
on the E A D and G strings for
at least six months. Then I discovered
a twelve-year-old could get a shiner
just for carrying a violin case
through Glendale Square, though
glen and *dale* sounded like places
hums and drones might emanate from.
Nearly seventy years later I'm hearing
fiddles Saturdays on the FM. Not violins,
fiddles that make me wish I'd stayed
with it, coaxing enough style from my sawing
that now I could be touring
both sides of the North Atlantic
with Malachy's Lads, or inventing
duets with Aurian Greene, or fiddling
in a circle with the Hardanger Navy.

VII

Rickety as I Am

All over Ireland you see them on side roads
and sheep farms, sometimes like clocks
held upside-down, one leg in the air,
out of joint or pointing at the flock,
some still after cars. Border collies,
and sometimes as you pass the master
will call out, "He couldn't drive it
if he caught it." When young
Lefty was that way, always ready
to give it a try on Castle Road or Corn Hill
until Charlotte appeared, a red-haired,
green-eyed girl one generation
from Skibbereen. But rickety as I am
and two generations from Ballinspittle
on the Old Head of Kinsale, I can only
approach her on two little wheels
and a couple of old tennis balls
to taste the muffin and brownie she leaves
as she and Lefty head for the road.

Those Backdrop Cities

Behind the pols and infamous others
interviewed on TV there are buildings
that resemble illuminated ladders
to Nowhere, or else rocketships
designed for an evil khan. Some have
rooftops that look like MD needles.
There is no birdspeak saluting the dawn
or driving the blue and gray skyrats
into the dark. Some of those backdrops
look like the Scandinavian *Duchess*
on a cruise sailed into a wrong left turn
and grounded on a foreign sidewalk.
There's no strand there to support
a string of wild ponies, either,
let alone enough soil for a skinny
foxglove to put down roots. Not that
I can afford it, but would I want
to live where it appears that
men in blue suits are shoveling
ragtime doubletalk at the questioners
and the leaves withhold their oxygen
from creatures that never tell a lie?

Porky's Boy

"You must be Porky's boy.
Do you play in the band?"
a man I had never seen before
asked me in the athletic building.
He gave me a look the local
Italians called the *malyuck*.

"Aw, no," my father said, "he's on
the football team." My father
was called Porky after another
guy named Porky, unrelated.

When I asked him at home
who the guy with the evil eye was,
he said, "That's your godfather
Jugga Callahan. Always a bottle
in his car." My father was Porky
all his life, though never fat
and never out loud by me.

In his old-age wheelchair, with
Lou Gehrig's disease (football
in the 1920s in a cardboard helmet),
I called him Clank, but never
to his face. Only Cabbage Head
Lawlor called me Porky's Boy then,

but thanks to Uncle P. P.
Marshmallow, a minor character
in a John Cheever novel, that's
who I thought myself to myself
with my enlarged prostate.

Envy

Night in the outskirts,
rut and dust, dead end.

Prickling weeds crowd
the dark green fence.

A house here once; now,
leaves like dry tongues

between the palings
someone kicked in.

Nobody comes. On the
splintery creosote pole

there's not even an old
barrel hoop backboard

to impede the climb
up spikes to the bulb

under the rippled tin
where the hot june bug

spins forever.

Under the Wolf Moon

It rises over the hill, the star Pollux nearby,
appears in the kitchen window after
polishing the stone of my love
of fifty years, beside whom I will lie
in the family resting place, that field
among friends and enemies, some
under boulders with plaques inscribed,
and a few painters who mattered.

That moon of flooding harbors
and extreme cold will measure me awhile
through rooftop glass before moving on
above the river, then to Pond Village
two miles away, where my grandfather
brought his children summers
after he thought the dunes looked like
Carndonagh and Trawbreaga Bay, Donegal.
Uncle Gilberto, born here, dove for whiting
as a kid, fifty cents a bucket, and later
for tourist coins off the wharf.

Under the wolf moon you may remember
everything. Though it may not roll a seaman
onto the beach at High Head tonight,
somewhere below its light a fisherman
is speaking Portuguese in his sleep.

I Will Not Die in Paris on a Thursday

I wouldn't swap the local red sandstone pillars
and heights inside St. Magnus's, Kirkwall,
or the Cistercian ruins at Corcomroe
for Notre Dame, so if you're looking for me
and I'm not corrupting the cemetery
in Truro, Massachusetts, forget Paris,

and having already been to Thor's river
and Thor's harbor, Muckle Flugga
and St. Molaga's house and bed, I'm probably
somewhere along the line my DNA took between
Malin Head and the Old Head of Kinsale.

Look for me in the north, where
the Donegal mountains allow loughs
and bays, and the Dohertys and McLaughlins
continue marrying forever. Or else in the far
south of Kilcolman and Ballinspittle

where the Sextons and Galvins lie together
after extreme unction, still in contempt
of the bitter fragments of fortresses
that stand like anorexia in stone
and long for the ground.

And come to think of it, in our own country
check Walter Anderson's painted walls
at Ocean Springs, Mississippi. Could the Louvre
light me up any better than his hunting cats
that set out and return under fluid spines,
or just one of his frogs or skinks?

Against Expendables

Because they cross hemispheres it is
always summer where the red knots fly.
They will not disappear into a new name
like the long-tailed duck, but in twenty years
a planet we are cooking may deal
the red knots a death blow.
Because of deeper tides the glaciers
are melting into, submerging the mussel spat
and eggs of horseshoe crabs whose sustenance
they once found by heart on beaches,
now the knots mis-time their northern flights.
In twenty years or less the four hundred surviving
right whales may be gone as well. Snowball,
a young adult named for his tail spots,
was found floating dead in the St. Lawrence gulf
on Tuesday, a regular visitor there
and everywhere between Florida and the Strait
of Belle Isle, a veteran of three severe
lobster gear entanglements and a ship strike.
On the nine thousand miles between Patagonia
and Greenland a red knot's heart lacking food
may shrink, and crash. Before any
Caribbean landfall, higher waters may mean
more sunken islands and eroded mudflats
where once the market gunners left their prints.
Will we blame this emptiness on ourselves?
When the shadows of the vultures'
ragged wings trawl over us, who will
offer forgiveness anywhere?

www.ingramcontent.com/pod-product-compliance
Lightning Source LLC
Chambersburg PA
CBHW022149090426
42742CB00010B/1439